TH_
LITTLE
BOOK
OF
TURNING
60

Welcome to the uproarious world of being 60!

This book is your passport to a club where memory is as selective as a gourmet food critic, fashion rules are made to be broken (mostly by socks and sandals), and 'Netflix and chill' often turns into 'nap and snack'.

So, fasten your seatbelts because this ride is a rollercoaster of laughs, forgetfulness, and an endless quest for the TV remote.

Cheers to turning 60—the age where wrinkles are just well-earned stripes and laughter is the best therapy.

"At 60, I've reached the age where I'm no longer looking for a silver lining; I'm looking for my keys."

"Turning 60 means my train of thought often leaves the station without me."

"Life at 60: When 'making new friends' means memorizing new doctors' names."

"*At 60, my hearing might be selective, but my memory's just picky.*"

"I've hit 60, where 'new friends' come with free medical advice and prune recipes."

"At 60, my phone's autocorrect is like my memory – often making things up."

"60 is the age where yoga pants and napping compete for the 'outfit of the day' award."

"Life begins at 60, where 'getting lucky' means finding the remote on the first try."

"At 60, my favorite exercise is a mix of walking and 'searching for things I've misplaced'."

"60 is the new 40—
just with 20 more
years of collecting
bad jokes."

"Turning 60 is like a rollercoaster: the only difference is that the ups and downs come from standing up too fast."

"At 60, my hobbies include giving unwanted advice and forgetting where I put my glasses."

"60: The age when I tell the same stories repeatedly, mainly because I forgot who already heard them."

"At 60, 'wild nights' are all about staying up past 9 PM."

"Life at 60: where my dancing is reserved for the kitchen and my audience is the cat."

"*60 is the age where 'feeling young' is having one less ache than yesterday.*"

"Turning 60 means my memory's like a broken record, but the cracks make the music of life."

"At 60, my idea of a night out is the joy of not having to set an alarm for the morning."

"60: Where 'getting lucky' is finding a sale on comfy shoes."

"Life at 60: where 'running late' means I'm not wearing my slippers yet."

"At 60, I've become a connoisseur of the 'look' that means I've misplaced something again."

"Life at 60: where 'high fashion' is all about finding pants with an elastic waistband."

"60: where 'exercise' is lifting the TV remote and reaching for the snacks simultaneously."

"At 60, my social life revolves around invitations to free blood pressure checks."

"Life at 60:
'charging up'
means more about
my devices than
my social energy."

"60 is when 'couch surfing' is less about adventure and more about a cozy Saturday afternoon."

"At 60, my annual check-up feels more like a performance review for my body."

"Life at 60: where 'weekend plans' are code for catching up on sleep."

"60 is the age where 'comfortable shoes' take priority over trendy ones."

"At 60, 'a good night out' involves a good book and a cup of herbal tea."

"*Life at 60: where 'multi-tasking' means remembering what day it is and what I went into the kitchen for.*"

"60: the age where I'm not 'aging'; I'm just adding more stories to my library of wrinkles."

"At 60, I've upgraded my collection of recipes: now it's all about making meals that won't upset my stomach."

"Life at 60: where 'let's go wild' translates to trying a new flavor of herbal tea."

"60 is the age where 'rocking out' is more about a rocking chair than a concert."

"At 60, 'flexibility' refers to my schedule, not my yoga poses."

"Life at 60: where 'Friday night lights' mean I forgot to turn them off before bed."

"60 is the age where 'happy hour' is about finding a peaceful hour in the day."

"At 60, my enthusiasm for technology is just as strong as my ability to accidentally pocket-dial."

"*Life at 60: where 'carpe diem' means seizing the opportunity to take a good nap.*"

"At 60, my memory is like my favorite playlist - it keeps shuffling without my consent."

"Life at 60: where 'getting lucky' means finding the last slice of pie in the fridge."

"60 is the age when 'Netflix and chill' translates to a comfortable sofa and a good book."

"At 60, I've mastered the skill of nodding and pretending I remember people's names."

"Life at 60: where 'nightlife' involves changing into pajamas at 7 PM."

"60 is the age where 'adventure' means trying a new flavor of oatmeal."

"At 60, 'small talk' is simply an opportunity to exercise my selective hearing."

"*Life at 60: where 'staying up late' means seeing the end credits of a movie.*"

"60: the age when a 'wild night out' is a walk through the neighborhood after dark."

"At 60, I've reached the level of expertise where I forget what I'm saying while I'm saying it."

"Life at 60: where 'turning heads' just means people are impressed by how well I parallel park."

"60 is the age where 'fashion statement' means finding the comfiest pair of slippers."

"At 60, my idea of a balanced diet involves chocolate in each hand."

"Life at 60: where 'being social' means interacting with the cashier at the grocery store."

"60 is the age where 'staying connected' means not misplacing your reading glasses."

"At 60, 'the daily grind' refers to making a perfect cup of coffee in the morning."

"Life at 60: where 'a night on the town' might involve stargazing from the backyard."

"60 is the age where 'pulling an all-nighter' is staying awake past 9 PM."

"At 60, I'm as spontaneous as a pre-planned retirement vacation."

"Life at 60: where 'embracing change' means upgrading to the latest model of comfy armchair."

"At 60, my dance moves are so old school they're back in style... in a history museum."

"Life at 60: where 'late night cravings' mean finding the cookies you stashed for emergencies."

"60 is the age where 'celebrating all night' refers to waking up just once for a bathroom break."

"At 60, I've perfected the art of selective memory - remembering only the good old days."

"Life at 60: where 'burning the midnight oil' involves accidentally leaving a nightlight on."

"60 is the age where 'living it up' means savoring a good cup of tea."

"At 60, I've upgraded my party tricks from juggling to balancing my retirement funds."

"*Life at 60: where 'keeping up with the Joneses' is about remembering the names of my neighbors.*"

"60: the age when 'happy hour' means finding a good sale at the grocery store."

"At 60, I've discovered that the best things in life aren't things - they're naps."

"Life at 60: where 'staying out late' involves watching the sunset from the porch."

"60 is the age where 'making plans' involves having multiple backup napping locations."

"At 60, I've reached the level of expertise where my most impressive dance move is not falling."

"Life at 60: where 'night owls' are the birds I hear outside my window."

"60 is the age where 'adrenaline rush' means finding a good sale on warm socks."

"At 60, my flexibility is about adjusting my plans, not my yoga poses."

"Life at 60: where 'seizing the day' involves savoring each morning's first cup of coffee."

"60 is the age where 'breakfast for dinner' is a rebellious act of living on the edge."

"At 60, I've upgraded from 'adulting' to 'senioring' – it involves napping and sensible footwear."

"Life at 60: where 'dancing the night away' is a marathon of changing TV channels."

"At 60, I've achieved 'expert level' in the sport of finding my glasses on top of my head."

"Life at 60: where 'spontaneity' is trying a new flavor of decaffeinated coffee."

"60 is the age where 'rocking out' is more about rocking in a rocking chair."

"At 60, my idea of 'burning calories' involves watching a marathon of cooking shows."

"Life at 60: where 'energy drinks' involve adding an extra sugar cube to my tea."

"60 is the age where 'unplanned adventures' refer to getting lost in my own neighborhood."

"At 60, I've mastered the 'disappearing act'— where items vanish when I'm holding them."

"Life at 60: where 'pulling an all-nighter' means staying up to watch the sunrise."

"60: the age when 'letting loose' is about finding the comfy pair of pajamas."

"At 60, I've realized that 'wild nights' are all about staying up past 10 PM."

"Life at 60: where 'embracing change' means finally deciding to change the TV channel manually."

"60 is the age where 'staying young at heart' means playing bingo with an enthusiastic spirit."

"At 60, 'dressing to impress' involves matching my socks... most of the time."

"Life at 60: where 'social butterflies' might involve real butterflies and a bird feeder."

"60 is the age where 'setting the world on fire' is just turning up the thermostat a little higher."

"At 60, I've become an 'expert' at forgetting what I was about to say, before I say it."

"Life at 60: where 'going wild' means enjoying a spontaneous game of Sudoku."

"60 is the age where 'wild side' means having dessert before dinner on occasion."

"At 60, my secret to happiness is 'low expectations'— then everything is a pleasant surprise!"

"Life at 60: where 'adventure' is finding a new, yet comfortable, way to sit in a recliner."

Printed in Great Britain
by Amazon